Recognition of the Obvious

Translation by Roy Melvyn

Recognition of the Obvious
The Lost Writings of Wu Hsin Vol. 4
By Roy Melvyn
Copyright 2011 Roy Melvyn

Summa Iru Publishing
Boulder, Colorado 80020

Forward

Trying to grasp the teachings of Wu Hsin is like trying to grasp the wind in the palm of your hand. While they are as refreshing and fragrant as a fresh breeze, they can also be as devastating as a wildfire.

Wu Hsin doesn't provide answers to the questions of life because life is its own answer. It is what-is. It moves, it flows, it breathes itself into and through everything.

Instead, the writings of Wu Hsin expose, without compromise, the fundamental misconception that there is something called an individual that needs to find something else outside of itself. Admittedly, the sense of being a separate individual feels very real and affects every part of that apparent experience. Wu Hsin makes it abundantly clear; however, that this is a state of contracted energy, a sense of having lost something unnamable.

It would therefore seem that the source of all unhappiness is the individual not getting/finding what it wants. Yet, this is not the problem. Wu Hsin ponders:

All suffering is personal.
In the absence of the person,
Where can suffering alight?

No amount of effort can ever bring anything other than more *me* searching for that which the *me* doesn't have, the end result only serving to reinforce the reference center: *me.*

In *Volume Four, Recognition of the Obvious,* Wu Hsin illuminates that all hopes of attainment, all efforts at becoming, ultimately avoid that which *me* most fears … its own absence.

This message is so simple it totally confounds the mind. Almost instantaneously, the mind says "Yes, but…………what about this, what about that?"

There is no 'yes, but'. You can't say 'yes' and continue with 'but'. If the 'yes' is a real 'yes', that releases the thing into nothingness and it is finished. If you say 'but', you are giving continuity to that dead structure of thought, past experience and future hope.

Wu Hsin puts it this way:

What is keeping one from being in one's natural state?
One is constantly moving way from oneself.
One wants to be happy;
One is dissatisfied with one's experiences of life.
One wants new ones.
One wants to perfect oneself,
To change oneself.
Trying to be something other than what one is, is
The going away from oneself.
It is the resistance to What-Is.
The desire to alter this you, is
The only energy that sustains it.
In the absence of this energy,
You cannot continue;
Then, the natural state shines effortlessly.

Appearances notwithstanding, it is really as simple as that. What is unnatural may obscure what is natural. But it doesn't negate it.

When you look at an Escher picture, it may all of a sudden seem to turn inside out. Nothing has changed in the picture, but something has shifted in your perception of it. At this point you could say everything has changed, or nothing has changed.

To see through these things, requires investigation. This is the real gift of Wu Hsin, the challenge to investigate the validity of all concepts and all beliefs. It is here that the seeing through takes place and the clarity occurs. Yet, this clarity also has its price:

One can't have a piece of It.
It is all or nothing.
One must make room;

It requires a lot of space.
Everything must go.

Brief Background

It is widely believed that Wu Hsin was born during the Warring States Period (403-221 BCE), postdating the death of Confucius by more than one hundred years.

This was a period during which the ruling house of Zhou had lost much of its authority and power, and there was increasing violence between states. This situation birthed "the hundred schools", the flourishing of many schools of thought, each setting forth its own concepts of the prerequisites for a return to a state of harmony. The two most influential schools were that of Confucius and the followers of Mozi ("Master Mo"), the Mohists. The latter were critical of the elitist nature and extravagant behaviors of the traditional culture. The philosophical movement associated with the Daodejing also was emerging at this time. Wu Hsin's style of Daoist philosophy developed within the context defined by these three schools and appears to be most heavily influenced by that latter. In addition, it most clearly contains the seeds of what would become Ch'an Buddhism in China or Zen in Japan.

Wu Hsin was born in a village called Meng, in the state of Song. The Pu River in which Wu Hsin was said to have fished was in the state of Chen which had become a territory of Chu. We might say that Wu Hsin was situated in the borderlands between Chu and the central plains—the plains centered around the Yellow River which were the home of the Shang and Zhou cultures. Certainly, as one learns more about the culture of Chu, one senses deep resonances with the aesthetic sensibility of the Daoists, and with Wu Hsin's style in particular.

If the traditional dating is reliable, Wu Hsin would have been a contemporary of Mencius, but one is hard pressed to find any evidence that there was any communication between them. The philosopher Gao Ming, although not a Daoist, was a close friend and stories abound of their philosophical rivalries.

Wu Hsin's work was significant for Daoist religious practitioners who often took ideas and themes from it for their meditation practice, as an example, Sima Chengzhen's 'Treatise on Sitting and Forgetting' (ca. 660 C.E.).

He offers a highly refined view of life and living. When he writes "Nothing appears as it seems", he challenges the reader to question and verify every belief and every assumption.

Brevity was the trademark of his writing style. Whereas his contemporaries were writing lengthy tomes, Wu Hsin's style reflected his sense that words, too, were impediments to the attainment of Understanding; that they were only pointers and nothing more. He would use many of the same words over and over because he felt that people needed to hear words repeatedly, until the Understanding was louder than the words.

His writings are filled with paradoxes, which cause the mind to slow down and, at times, to even stop. Reading Wu Hsin, one must ponder. However, it is not an active pondering, but a passive one, much in the same way as one puts something in the oven and lets it bake for a while.

He repeatedly returns to three key points. First, on the phenomenal plane, when one ceases to resist What-Is and becomes more in harmony with It, one attains a state of Ming, or clear seeing. Having arrived at this point, all action becomes wei wu wei, or action without action (non-forcing) and there is a working in harmony with What-Is to accomplish what is required.

Second, as the clear seeing deepens (what he refers to as the opening of the great gate), the understanding arises that there is no one doing anything and that there is only the One doing everything through the many and diverse objective phenomena which serve as Its instruments.

From this flows the third and last: the seemingly separate me is a misapprehension, created by the mind which divides everything into pseudo-subject (me) and object (the world outside of this me). This seeming two-ness (dva in Sanskrit, duo in Latin, dual in English), this feeling of being separate and apart, is the root cause of unhappiness.

The return to wholeness is nothing more than the end of this division. It is an apperception of the unity between the noumenal and the phenomenal in much the same way as there is a single unity between the sun and sunlight. Then, the pseudo-subject is finally seen as only another object while the true Subjectivity exists prior to the arising of both and is their source.

All five volumes consist of what would appear to be his day-to-day reflections as they spontaneously arose. There is no progression in the pages, no evolution of the concepts put forth. As such, reading pages randomly or from the beginning has the same efficacy. Nor should it be read with haste; a page or two at a time is sufficient to allow for the content to sink in, as a thrown stone falls to the bottom of the lake.

In its essence, this book is a collection of hooks; any one of them is sufficient to catch a thirsty fish

Translator's Note

Material of this nature is not served well by language. It may seem that there are anomalies and contradictions. So, it is important to state that the translation of Wu Hsin's words herein is not purely literal. Instead, it contains an interpretation of what was clearly implied, and this is where the limitation of words is quite evident.

Compounding this problem, I have chosen to incorporate certain words into the translation which may appear to be incongruent relative to the time of Wu Hsin's writing.

The clearest example of this would be my use of the word ego which wasn't to come into being for many of hundreds of years after Wu Hsin's death.

I have done this to best capture the real essence of the intention behind the word. The original Chinese word 个人 (ge ren) means the individual. However, using the individual doesn't capture the sense of separateness that is better conveyed by ego.

The Sanskrit language also provides us with some marvelous insight. In it, the word for mind is manas, which translated literally means that which measures and compares. That says it pretty well. The Sanskrit word for ego is ahamkara; its translation is *I am the doer*. Within the context of Wu Hsin's message, the conveyance of the idea of I am the doer is vitally important. As such, this and other small liberties that I have taken with the translation feel more than reasonable.

RM

Volume Four: Recognition of the Obvious

Text

The first thought is I.
It is the root-thought,
The foundation upon which
All else is built and from which
All other thoughts have their origin.
The arrival of the I-thought and
The arrival of the world
Occur simultaneously.
Neither exists without the other.
This is Wu Hsin's open secret.
Those that make it their own
Move beyond struggle and strife,
Pleasure and pain.
To discard this is to
Throw away the diamonds with the ice.

*****

Awareness is the primal constant.
On it, worlds are built and
Individuals are imagined.

*****

Clarity is the great neutralizer.

*****

Thinking is not the natural state.
Perceiving thought is the natural state.
The pure perceiving is prior to
The imposition of a perceiver.

*****

There are some
Who are afraid of
Stepping outside of their huts,
Afraid of what they'll find.
More are there
Who are afraid of
Stepping outside of their minds.
Afraid that they'll find nothing when
They look back.

*****

One can feel miserable on
A beautiful beach.
One can feel ecstatic
While in jail.
The outer need not
Dictate the inner.
When the wall between the two dissolves,
That which sources both is revealed.

*****

When man wants to
Run away from the potential
Contained within him,
He creates his god to aspire to.
Wu Hsin declares:
They are not two.

*****

The personal world is
A reflection of the person.
What madness it is
To fault the reflection!
Can an image be changed without
Changing the face?

It is only ideas that
Create the notion of separation.
When it is seen that
Everything rises and sets in you,
What can you be separate from?

*****

The vision of unity is
The end of all things personal.
There is no event that
Delivers this unity vision.
Who could it occur to?
With nobody here and
Nobody there,
Everything is as it should be.

*****

All disappointment,
All disillusionment is
An invitation to investigate
Who is disappointed;
Who is disillusioned?

*****

The work of this moment is
Watching the work of this moment.

*****

Focusing on the plot of the book
Does not bring one
Closer to the author.

Where the where is not,
When the when is not,
I am.
In every experience,
The expression is
The objective part, which is changing.
The background is
The subjective part;
The unchanging field.

*****

That which is by its nature restless
Can never find peace.
Peace of mind is
The mind's fantasy.

*****

When it is seen that
An empty cup is receptive and
A full cup cannot receive,
Those with wisdom choose emptiness.

To be natural
Requires no learning.

*****

Stop pretending that what isn't is
Superior to What-Is.
It isn't.

*****

Either one is
Responsible for everything or
One is responsible for nothing.
The end result is the same.

Wang asked Wu Hsin:
"When shall I achieve this clarity?"
Wu Hsin replied,
"When the when is dead".

*****

Ignorance is the
Ignoring of what is
Clear, present, and obvious.
If the cloth fits, wear it.

*****

As soon as your god is assigned attributes,
It becomes merely another object in
A world of objects.
Only the non-objective god is
The true subject.

*****

The desire for salvation is
The elixir of fools.
The only saving one needs is to be
Saved from one's imagination.

The way the world appears is
Dependent on which side of the window
One is looking from.

*****

If the person is
Merely an appearance, then
Who cares?

Until one becomes clear about
The true source of happiness.
All looking for it is folly.

*****

The past is only a memory.
The future is only a hope.
All that matters is the present:
This-Here-Now.

*****

Whatever one perceives is not one's own.
It is merely an appearance in
The field of knowing that one is.

*****

Do not argue that
Your god is indifferent to you.
It is not indifference.
It is merely non-compliance.

*****

The body changes but
The I that claims its ownership does not.
The mind changes but
The I that claims its ownership does not.
The personality changes but
The I that claims its ownership does not.
It is solely of this I that
Wu Hsin speaks.

Eons could be spent
Talking about the seeming differences.
But they are not as they seem.
Seeing this is the
End of talking about it.

*****

All methods bind.
Those who are free
Hold to no system,
No regimen.

*****

The release of habitual activity,
Habitual reactivity,
Frees the individual
From the self-referencing center,
From the individual.

*****

There are no answers to be
Found out there.

*****

Perceiving sees everything whereas
Labeling only captures
A limited canvas.
The mind is the great labeler.

*****

Before the body,
Before the mind,
Are you not there?

Fragments trying to understand
That which has no fragmentation is
A great comedy.
The birth of me is
The birth of other than me……..
And so the game begins.

*****

What makes the wise wise?
Nothing more than seeing
The One appearing as the many.
Seeing through the appearance is everything.

*****

Seeking ends when the fish
Understand the folly of
Searching for the ocean.

*****

Embrace, my child, that which
You seek to avoid;
The fear of absence.
Absence of concepts,
Absence of ideas,
Absence of anyone to have them.
To be fully present therefore requires that
One be fully absent.
This is the Great Emptying.

Wu Hsin gives you the key.
Either you use it
To open the door or
You put it in your pocket with
All the other keys
You have accumulated.

Seeing through the haze of the personal,
One's actions are no longer reactions.

*****

To differentiate between
The guests and the host is to
Understand the distinction between
What comes and goes and
What is permanent.

*****

When one becomes water,
One's thirst is quenched.

*****

Wu Hsin did not come from somewhere.
He is not going anywhere.
He is timeless, prescient being itself.
When circumstances require his appearance,
Wu Hsin appears.
Give up all ideas of
What you believe yourself to be,
Then, you are he.

*****

One is not born with an identity.
Identity is acquired.
In the absence of all acquisitions,
True being shines.

There is great frustration in
Trying to locate
That which is non-local.
Many refer to this as searching.
Yet, one need not go anywhere
To find the Great Immediate.

*****

Mark your territory.
Construct as many signs as you wish declaring
This is Mine.
They are nothing but mist, because
The one who declares is also
Nothing but mist.

*****

Insight is the eradication of confusion.
No longer equating the way things seem with
The way things are,
Life is the ever-fresh awareness of being.
In this, the shadow cannot be
Mistaken for the substance.

*****

The sense of feeling separate
Need not be rejected.
It, too, is part of the Oneness.

*****

The difficulty with trying to
Remove false perceptions is that
One is creating them in every moment.
In openness, the drive to interpret is stilled and
Clarity arises to the forefront.

There can be knowledge of changes.
But, there cannot be
Knowledge of the Changeless.
Knowing the Changeless is
Being the Changeless.

*****

Looking in at
What is looking out,
Ends all seeking and
The seeker.

*****

There are no conditions that
Must be satisfied in order for
Insight to arise.
Nothing to do,
Nothing to become.

*****

Holiness is not wholeness.

*****

The events of the world
Do not impact Wu Hsin.
He is neither happy nor sad.
His happiness has a different aroma;
It is latent in his very being.

*****

Ultimately, one does not get free.
Instead, one realizes that
One is freedom itself.

All suffering is personal.
In the absence of the person,
Where can suffering alight?

*****

The character in a book cannot
Write the book in which he appears.
Investigate whether you are
The author or the character.

*****

As heat is inherent in fire, so too is
Knowing inherent in being.
This is the Knowing from where
I know erroneously arises.

*****

Wu Hsin tells you nothing that
You don't already know.
He only reminds you of that which
You have forgotten.
You may experience Wu Hsin as
Outside of yourself, yet truly
This is not the case.

*****

In the absence of
The addiction to content,
The mind is restored to
Purity and clarity.
Seeing, hearing, tasting, smelling,
Touching, feeling and thinking
Continue to operate without
Anyone to initiate them.
Natural functioning occurs with ease.
Life continues its flow.

When matters are seen clearly,
It is no longer important if
All the pieces fit.

*****

More.
More peace,
More beauty,
More harmony,
More pigs,
More rice,
More.
More is not the answer.

*****

Nowhere to go,
Nothing to do,
Nothing to get.
What could be simpler?

*****

The whole house is on fire.
You can only take
What you can carry.
The lighter you travel,
The farther you go.

*****

Clarity does not provide answers.
It dissolves questions.

No new systems,
New methods need be created.
Sweeping away the hindrances is enough.
It is then that the awareness of being,
Of being aware,
Radiates and illuminates the landscape.

*****

This I that one thinks one is, is
Merely a survival mechanism for
The form it is associated with.
The unstained apperception of this
Facilitates the return to
What is prior to all I's.
It is here that resting in being occurs.

*****

Try as one may,
One can't squeeze
A restless mind into
A peaceful space.
Recognize mind for what it is and
For what it is not, and
Neutrality is effortlessly established.

*****

Understanding has been
Clouded by misunderstanding.
The sun remains present in both
The absence and the presence of the clouds.
To see through the clouds is
To see the sun.

To be present and aware is not a state.
It is the ground from where
All states arise.
You are That.

*****

Beliefs can be as formative as
A fortress wall.
Unless the wall is torn down or surmounted,
One can't reach the other side.

*****

Trust neither scripture nor the sage
To provide the truth.
All truth must be self-investigated and is
Therefore, self-generated.

*****

If you must search,
Search for what
Needs to be given up.

*****

In open vibrancy,
The sight of a flower is as marvelous as
A vision of a god.

*****

Mu Ding held no ideas about
What perfection was; for him,
Every moment was therefore perfect.

No beginning.
No ending.
No birth.
No death.
No time.
No space.
Nowhere to leave.
Nowhere to arrive.
Home.

*****

The fundamental nature of things is
Unitary wholeness,
Oneness.
Separateness is a seeming,
An appearance,
Nothing more.

*****

Peace is present in every moment.
Remove the shroud of thought.
Where can peace not be found?

*****

To attempt to retain what was or
To attempt to attain what might be is
The source of all suffering.

*****

To find your self,
Explore your self.

Religions arise to address
The sense of being separate and apart.
Once this sense is seen to be erroneous,
Where is the need for religion?

*****

With lucidity,
Both the chaos and the randomness
Become quite orderly.

*****

Every moment spent in
The absence of presence is
A moment irretrievably lost.

*****

Know what you are not and
Be what you are.

*****

All pursuits,
All searches,
Takes one away from the natural state,
That state in which one always is.
*****

All are here, yet
You ask Wu Hsin
How to get here.
Why, then, are you
Disappointed by his silence?

What is keeping one from being in one's natural state?
One is constantly moving way from oneself.
One wants to be happy;
One is dissatisfied with one's experiences of life.
One wants new ones.
One wants to perfect oneself,
To change oneself.
Trying to be something other than what one is, is
The going away from oneself.
It is the resistance to What-Is.
The desire to alter this you, is
The only energy that sustains it.
In the absence of this energy,
You cannot continue;
Then, the natural state shines effortlessly.

*****

Why does one communicate with oneself?
Why is there thought?
If one does not communicate with oneself,
One is not there, absent.
One's absence is the primal fear.

*****

One is either the personal or
The awareness of the personal.
No act of volition can take one from
The former to the latter.

*****

The need for time is
The need for practice.
The time bound can never
Yield the timeless.

Those who let the intelligent energy
Express itself in its own way are
Those who Wu Hsin calls clear.
There is nothing they need do.
There is nothing they need not do.

*****

Those who ask Wu Hsin
The meaning of life
Need to first become alive.
There, the question and the questioner
Dissolve in the aliveness.
The purpose of the flower is to flower.
The purpose of man is to flower.
No difference.

*****

Whatever one does
To free oneself from oneself is merely
More of oneself.

*****

Stop talking and thinking.
Therein, nothing can remain unknown.

*****

To pursue appearances is to
Ignore the source of appearances.

*****

The entryway to the Unknown is narrow.
One must set aside all acquired knowledge so that
One may gain access.

It is only when one is awake that
One can know one was asleep.

*****

To obtain this Understanding to which
Wu Hsin refers,
One must discard everything
One finds along the way.

*****

Choosing that which is safe,
That which is predictable, is
The surest way to go nowhere.
 Let us be clear:
One doesn't know what is good;
One knows only what is good for oneself.
What is bad for the field mouse is
Good for the satiated owl.

*****

It is preferable to
Investigate one's assumptions than it is to
Attempt to solve one's problems.

*****

One thinks oneself to be the dancer.
In fact, one is the dancing.

*****

Wu Hsin can no more help one
Find one's god than he can
Help the bird find the sky.

Take hold of any sentence Wu Hsin speaks.
Shake it well until
All the words drop off.
Drink deeply from that which remains.

*****

Silence is not the absence of sound.
Silence is the absence of you.

*****

Can throwing white paint at the sky
Make the sky white?
Those who are vibrant and clear are
Unaffected by appearances in the world.

*****

Change your clothes.
Change your name.
What you are is untouched.

*****

The journey of self-discovery ends with
The discovery that there is no self.

*****

True courage brushes aside
Everything experienced,
Everything felt, and
Everything known.
The soil is then ready for
The arrival of the unknown.

No labels are applicable.
No categories can be referenced.
The words of Wu Hsin cannot be
Contained within any container.
If one constructs a box to put them in,
There has been a misunderstanding.

*****

One wants to be different,
Sometime in the future, from
What one is today.
Full acceptance of What-Is is
The end of the future.

*****

You have arrived.
Soon, you will leave because
What you chase after
Cannot be found here.
It is not an object.
How then, can it be found,
Here or anywhere?

*****

The tricks played by
That which demands continuity can be very subtle.
When continuity loses its importance,
That which demanded it exists no longer.

*****

Understanding is the end of questions.
If one understands,
One is quiet.

One can't have a piece of It.
It is all or nothing.
Make room;
It requires a lot of space.
Everything must go.

*****

Who cares about death
Once there is recognition of the
Falseness of the individual?
Seeing the falseness is the death.

*****

The words of Wu Hsin will
No longer matter when
One becomes fully attentive to
His silence.

*****

Everything is falling.
To attach oneself to anything neither
Halts nor slows one's descent.

*****

What one needs comes when
One doesn't ask for
What one doesn't need.

*****

To be certain of the immediate
Precludes the attainment of the Ultimate.

Why are so many
So willing to exchange
Peace for thoughts?

*****

The final step is
The giving up of
All steps.

*****

Nothing new need be
Added or found.
Dig away the earth and
The pit is no longer hidden.

*****

To live in authentic wakefulness is to
Do one thing at a time and
To do it totally.

*****

One can't search for
Something to acquire while
Dropping all acquisitions.
When it is seen that
The searching does not bear fruit,
The dropping can begin.

*****

Wrong ideas obscure What-Is.
Loosen their hold and
Living becomes natural and easy.

Make room for understanding.
But remember that
Making room isn't
Bringing something in from elsewhere.

*****

One is not in the world;
The world is in oneself.
The parchment is not the writing.
Yet, without it,
There is no message.
The world is because
One is.

*****

The floodgates of insight
Open of their own accord.
No one to do it;
Nothing to be done.

*****

The sword can never understand dueling;
Nor can the fire-pit understand cooking.

*****

An elegant structure has been built.
Until it is torn down,
Nothing changes......................
And never confuse being
An instrument of change with being
An agent of change.

What effort can succeed in
Stopping the shaking of the reflection of
The tree on the lake?

*****

Harmonious and disharmonious are
Merely points of view whereas
Friction is a natural occurrence.
Being neither good nor bad,
It transcends opinion.
What happens isn't the problem
Analyzing what happens is the problem.

*****

Individuality implies ownership:
My thoughts,
My fear,
My body.
Seen clearly, there are thoughts.
There are fears,
There is a body but
There is no one they happen to.

*****

Chin Ho was called a simpleton.
He did not see right and wrong.
He could not judge good from bad.
He smiled too much.
The simple life is not
The life of a simpleton.
Yet, this simplicity is too complex for
Comprehension by many.

Pursuing anything that
Comes and goes cannot
Yield integral perception.
It is the seeing through what
Comes and goes that
Yields integral perception.

*****

The apperception of What-Is can
Only be achieved by
The elimination of
The obstacles to What-Is.
Wu Hsin cannot describe What-is.
He can only describe what is not.
The elimination of what is not is
The Great Unlearning.

*****

The source of all unhappiness is fragmentation.
Breaking the whole into parts,
Pitting one against the other,
Feeling apart and alone.
No restoration is required.
When it becomes obvious that
The fragmentation is erroneous,
It loses its power.

*****

There is no middle ground.
Reject everything or
Accept everything.
The result is the same.

There exists an inherent tension between
That which is personal and
That which is impersonal.
The desire to transcend the personal
Arises from the impersonal.
Since that which is personal would
Never agree to its own demise,
Who will bring about the transcendence?

*****

Whereas me is always changing,
I never changes.
Whereas me is always feeling threatened,
I is never threatened.
When one becomes unselfconscious,
There is no one
Other than I.

*****

When the world is viewed from neutrality,
Without fragmentation and
In the absence of a self centered perspective,
There arises an appreciation of
The beauty and perfection of What-Is.

*****

True peace is without cause.
Likewise, true happiness is without cause.
Conditioning these on any thing is
A movement away from them.

*****

There is a single requirement:
Don't run away.

Freedom from all content is
The precursor to
The knowledge of content.
You are That.

*****

Do not add even a single concept.
One must be emptied.
Only when one is empty of
The emptiness too,
Can the fullness manifest.

*****

Monolithic structures are built to
Provide a ground beneath one's feet, to
Provide safety and solidity.
These structures are not real.
Seeing this, how real are safety and solidity?

*****

Unity is the release of
The superstition of plural spirits.

*****

Seeing the finite is not enough.
Seeing the infinite in the finite is
Seeing without a seer.
Here, the seeing is being.

*****

Those who refuse to be what they are will
Remain what they are not.

Hell is living on the periphery.
It is where fixation on stories is
The preferred substitute to living.

*****

Most have difficulty seeing clearly because
Their heads are in the way.

*****

For all, life has a beginning,
A middle and an end.
However, it need not necessarily
Occur in that order.

*****

Causes produce effects which are
In themselves, new causes.

*****

What one comes to Wu Hsin to get,
One does not get.
Wu Hsin only gives
What one already is.

*****

When true emptiness is met,
Face to face,
Everything is lost.
What remains is what one is.

*****

Flow around obstacles.
Don't confront them, unless
The obstacle is oneself.

Before desiring to become something else,
Inquire fully into what you presently are.
What is seen is that
There is nowhere to come from and
Nowhere to go to.

*****

The immediacy is that there is presence-awareness.
All else that ensues is a story.

*****

When one is enamored with the means,
One becomes forgetful of the ends.
Once the cart has arrived,
One doesn't continue to sit in it.

*****

Call it emptiness or
Call it fullness.
It doesn't matter.
Its achievement rests on
Giving up one's relationship
With one's erroneous viewpoints.

*****

Don't look at Wu Hsin's finger.
Look at where it points to.

*****

Right here,
Right now, is
All that there is.
Immersed in thought,
One misses it.

When one changes,
Everyone changes and
The world changes.

*****

One must not confuse
What is innate from
What is acquired.
Divide the two,
Reject the latter and
Be.
 The personalization of the functioning is the error.
There is thinking with no thinker.
There is doing with no doer.

*****

Words.
At the spoken level,
They are sounds.
At the subtle level,
They are thoughts.
At the silent level,
They are gone.
It is in this silence,
From this silence, that
All arises.

*****

The need for gods decreases as
Awareness increases.

To be dissatisfied,
One must think about it.
To be unhappy,
One must think about it.
To find out what one truly is,
One must inquire prior to thought.
See things as Wu Hsin sees them and
Your hands will be in the earth while
Your head is in the sky.

*****

The body is insentient.
It cannot speak.
It cannot see.
It cannot think.
That which energizes the body,
That which initiates all action,
You are That.

*****

Wu Hsin is little more than
An open window through which
A cool breeze blows.
Nothing more.

*****

Once the true center is perceived,
There is no longer a need for enemies.

*****

The lack of concern for progress is
The only sign of progress.

All unhappiness is
Sourced from unexamined beliefs.

*****

The landscape toward clear neutrality is
Littered with identities and labels.

*****

This heavy garment,
This personal identity,
Seems to protect.
It is merely a second skin,
One step removed from the infinite.
Take it off and
Move beyond all need for protection.

*****

In the transpersonal life,
The middleman is removed.
Life is lived directly.

*****

Cling to no method,
No path and,
No teacher.
The rope that rescues one from the raging river
Can also be used to hang oneself.

*****

As the voice requires its distinctive tone,
Being requires a distinctive way of being.
Wu Hsin calls this you.

There is no need to
Go beyond the mind.
Seeing through it will suffice.

Wu Hsin does not speak about religion.
What is religion but
The transformation of
The song of liberation into
The dogmas of limitation?

*****

The Great Mystery cannot be understood.
It is the answer to the question:
What color is the wind?

*****

Emptiness,
Silence,
Stillness.
This is not a void to be feared but
A sanctuary to be sought.

*****

The cage door is open right now.
Wu Hsin cannot walk through it for you.

*****

First, you will strive to get it.
Then, you will strive to keep it.
Once lost, you will strive to reclaim it.
This is the wheel of striving.
Its grip is tight, but
It is you that must let go.

No action is self-generated.
The source of the action remains unseen,
Cloaked in its mysteriousness.
Observation of it is enough.
Many days of silence are required to
Recover from the futility of words.

*****

When the unacceptable is
No longer accepted,
Wu Hsin is sought out.

*****

Spontaneous living is
Devoid of musts.
 The two sides of the stick are
Awareness on the one side and
The habitual and mechanical on the other.

 *****

Whatever it is:
Happiness or unhappiness,
Joy or sorrow,
Comfort or discomfort,
Let it be.
It arrived without permission and
It will go in like fashion.

*****

That which perceives the world cannot be
Found in the world because
It is the world.

Death for the caterpillar is
Birth for the butterfly.
Form yields to form.
And so it goes.

Deep wisdom is not derived from experience.
It is derived from seeing clearly
The limitations of experience.

*****

The pure I becomes the thought
I am, which expands to
Become I am this.
This is the Great Unfolding.

*****

Deep looking produces
Deep seeing.
Then, one moves from competing to
Cooperating with everything.

*****

To be free,
One must untie oneself from
The seeming independent entity called me.

*****

Throwing away reactions,
One lives responsively,
Doing what is needed
When it is needed.

There is nothing to manage,
No persons,
No situations,
No things and
No one to manage them.

The common man is blind.
He cannot see
The nothingness that birthed him.
Nor can he see
The infinity that envelops him.

*****

Being requires no declaration,
Neither affirmation nor validation.
Who is it who declares
I am not?

*****

Mu Lai's house was ransacked by burglars.
A beautiful rug was stolen.
It took Mu Lai many days before
He could see the floor.
Before that, all he could see was
The absence of the rug.

*****

How can one experience life when
One is so busy becoming?

*****

Acceptance of What-Is cannot be
Created by the will.
The recognition of this is
The acceptance itself.

Those who don't know,
Believe.

One need not use
The candle of another.
One's own light is sufficient.

*****

That which gives rise to all forms is
Formlessness itself.
To create a picture of it in the mind is
Like catching a moth;
The body is held but
The beauty of the flight is eluded.

*****

Until one is willing to question that which
One is afraid to question,
There can be no movement.

*****

The word fire cannot burn.
Nor can the word water be consumed.
When one's vision is unobstructed,
There is no confusing
The description and the described.

*****

Being and becoming cannot walk together.

Seeing things as they are,
In the absence of interpretation, is
The end of the trance.

*****

Nothing to accumulate.
Nothing to acquire.
Nothing to gain.
Remove the non-essential; then
The essential essence itself shines.

*****

Heaven and hell are only
Lodgings for individuals.
When the fiction of individuals is seen through,
Heaven and hell lose all meaning.
Nothing to do,
Nowhere to go;
Now or later.
 Once the silence is established,
True listening can begin.

*****

The natural state is not an effect.
It has no cause.
It shines through
All causes and effects and
Precedes them.

*****

Transcendence is not
The disappearance of the transcended.
It is the natural refusal to
Attend to the transcended.

In the Great Awakening,
There is perfect
Adaptation and response to whatever comes.
The life, as such, is lived.

Timeless, spaceless, imperceptible being is
What one is.
Temporal, finite,
Sensorially perceptible phenomena are
What one appears to be.
This is the entire matter.
Yet, do not seek to grasp it or
It will be lost.

*****

The Ultimate Subject is revealed in
The cessation of objectification and identification.

*****

The mind thinks.
But it does not know.
Before the thinking mind,
Perceiving senses,
Doing body,
Happy or unhappy person,
The knowing stands.

*****

In seeing things as they are,
Where is the need for managing,
Controlling or manipulating?
To live naturally is to
Live without an agenda.

Hell is life on the periphery.

*****

Fresh understandings are obtained by
Questioning one's unassailable beliefs.
Clearer and clearer one becomes until
One is clarity itself.

*****

One can't learn to swim from
The luxury of one's armchair.

*****

The recognition of what is
Fundamental in oneself
Saps the power from the notion of
Being an individual.
Management and control of externals ceases.
Living continues.

*****

All that one has is this moment and
It is quite enough.

*****

In the absence of right and wrong,
What can be the problem?

*****

The effort to be made is
The same effort one made to
Grow from a fetus into
What one appears to be.

To lose the personal is to
Gain the totality of the universe.
This is living in ease,
Absent any need for improvement in character.

*****

The Knowing of which Wu Hsin speaks is not an activity.
It ever was and is and has never changed as
The support of all activity.

*****

Wholeness has never been broken;
It only seems that way.

*****

The mind cannot do anything except
Extend the frontiers of its own ignorance.
One cannot use the mind to
Transcend the mind.

*****

The I that claims ownership of
The body, mind, and senses is
The true Subjective.
It points back to one's true nature.

*****

Deep peace resides at the center.
Excursions away from the center are
Excursions away from peace.

One need not wait to be
What one already is.
Keeping the attention fixed on
What is permanent,
One can never stray.

*****

The setting of a goal is
The death of spontaneity.
Being aware of being aware is enough.

*****

Don't believe in
Anything you are asked to believe in.
Question everything until
All that remains is to
Question the questioner.

*****

All experience occurs in the field of time.
As such, the timeless can never be experienced.
All searching for experiences can now end.

*****

Taking the actions of Totality to be one's own is
The error in viewpoint.
As long as one is mesmerized by the tree,
The root cannot be understood.

*****

Live in accordance with
One's inherent nature.
What more can one do,
When, in truth, there is no doer?

It is only resistance that impedes acceptance.
As the dam impedes the river's flow,
Resistance impedes the flow of What-Is.
To drop all resistance is
To embrace What-Is,
Just as it is,
Without it having to be
Other than it is.
All of life is then welcomed.

*****

What one thinks one is, is
The result of inattention.
With attention, one attains
Clarity of thought,
Charity of feeling,
Purity of action and
The understanding of
The true nature of things.

*****

Questioning how to live
Misses the mark.
It is better to inquire
What is it that is living?

*****

Let us be clear;
The mind is merely
The name of a function:
Thinking.
In the absence of thought,
There is no mind.

One perceives objects through the senses.
One perceives the senses through the mind.
One perceives the mind by oneself.
It is only this oneself that is to be sought.
It is not hard to find.
Its fragrance is everywhere and
Pervades every thing.

*****

The unsatisfactory nature of the world
Must be acknowledged.
The futile attempts to
Make the unsatisfactory satisfactory
Must be acknowledged.
Only then, can alternatives be considered.
Of these, the best alternative is
The acceptance of What-Is.
In such acceptance,
All notions of satisfaction and dissatisfaction vanish
What remains is peace.

*****

Here and now is
All that there is.
It is What-Is.
The rest is imagination.

*****

The way outward into the world is with
The emphasis of objects.
The return inward from the world is with
The emphasis on the Subject.

Since one can perceive
One's body, senses and mind,
One stands separate from them as
Perceiving itself.

*****

To attempt to capture
The true essence of Wu Hsin is to
Try to observe the unobservable.
It is here that words fail.
The senses fail.
The Knowing of it is all.

*****

All notions of individuality are
Notions of ownership:
My body,
My thoughts,
My feelings.
Even when the error is apperceived,
It is apperceived by no one.

*****

The first step is to
Tear up the map.
This is the departure from
The known to the unknown.

*****

All there is is
Never not here,
Never not now.

One gets further lost in
All destinations other than
Here.

*****

One is either cramped or
One is open.
Whereas there may be degrees of cramped,
There are no degrees of open.

*****

To free oneself
From oneself requires
The investigation into
The reality of this self.
From here arises freedom.
Freedom from this and that,
Freedom from yes and no.
Freedom to be
What one has always been,
Before one was someone.

*****

The notion that
Something needs to be added is
A subtle form of postponement.
It feeds the idea of becoming
In the space where no becoming is required.

*****

There must be no waiting for
Something to happen.
This something is happening in every moment.
To wait for it is to miss it.

From the personal point of view,
The world is external to the personal.
When this dissolves like ice in water,
It is seen that nothing is external.
Everything is contained within the unified whole.
There is no separate person.
One is because the world is.
The world is because one is.
Arising and setting together,
Where is the boundary between them?
Use the mind to attain the
Point of understanding that
The answer is not in the mind.
Therein, the searching ends.

*****

The sum of all thoughts form another thought, me.
From there springs
A series of thoughts,
Reactions to thoughts,
That are thoughts themselves and are in essence
Preferences, rejections, wishes and longings.
The cycle of this complex is endless.
Its transcendence resides in
Returning to the condition
Prior to the first thought.
This is the clear space that the wise know.

*****

Even assigning It a name is too much.

*****

It is said that
Wu Hsin is greedy.
He gives nothing and
Takes everything.

Where is the location that
Inside becomes outside?
Where does here become there?
What distinguishes you from
Other than you?
Show Wu Hsin the markers,
The signposts and the boundaries.

*****

Being is being as one is,
Being as one was and
Being as one will be.
No difference.

*****

Life cannot be understood unless
One takes the time to observe it.
This observation must
Begin with and from the reference point:
Me.

*****

So much is found after
The cessation of seeking.

*****

The essence of Wu Hsin's words cannot be
Captured by the mind.
This is like trying to
Capture sunshine in a box.

One is not any thing in particular.
All one really is is
The denial of everything that
One is not;
The Eternal Constant.

*****

Failing to see the essence,
The pot but not the clay,
The bangle but not the silver,
The writing but not the parchment,
One remains ensnared in appearances,
Taking the way things seem for
The way things are.

*****

Union is only necessary
When separation is imagined.
When separation is seen to be imaginary,
The need for union drops off.

*****

Let there be no confusion between
Being an instrument of action and
The author of action.
In so doing,
The natural state remains unobscured.

*****

Others see differences between
Themselves and Wu Hsin whereas
Wu Hsin sees none.
Others believe that
Wu Hsin has what they lack.
Wu Hsin laughs at this.

One may read scripture until
The day one dies, yet
One can never drink water from
The map of a lake.

*****

Many there are who
Believe in making sacrifices to their gods.
To these, Wu Hsin notes that
The highest sacrifice is
The sacrifice of one's absolute certainties.

*****

The need to see magic births,
The appearance of magicians.
When even the miraculous is
Understood to be normal and ordinary,
What-Is is clearly discerned.

*****

Wu Hsin offers no hope,
No payoff,
No methodology and
No escape route.
Only the bravest are willing to
Confront their own absence.

*****

Those looking for answers must
Look where the answer resides.
You are That.

Let us not confuse beliefs with facts.
Your god is a belief.
You are is a fact.
Hold to the facts.

*****

Don't deny existence to
What can't be imagined.
Don't assert existence for
What is already imagined.
This is the creation of spaciousness wherein
True seeing occurs.

*****

One knows that one is.
One knows not what one is.
When it is seen that
What one is is no thing,
The seeking and the sought are no more.

*****

The wise have investigated the remainders:
The clarity that remains
When the mental chatter ceases.
The silence that remains when
The external noises ebb.
The presence that remains when
The past and the future are forsaken.
It may be said that
They recede into the background.
In truth, they comprise the Background.

*****

One stands at the threshold,
A single thought away from perfection.

Outside of the cage,
One is not someone who is free.
Rather, one is freedom itself.

*****

Whatever appears before you
Cannot be you.

*****

The vista, the viewpoint expands.
Suddenly, there is no elsewhere,
There is no there.
There is only Here onto which
Things come and go.
The Here remains.
Occurring right now,
It is a singular, undivided tapestry.

*****

Words are the great trap.
If the mind becomes ensnared there,
One can never get free.

*****

Insight arrives unbidden.
It is sired by neither prayer nor ritual.
In silent spaciousness,
It shouts its message.

*****

One is never apart from one's destination.
When the questioning of the dream begins,
Awakening is not far away.

The mind, the body, and the world are
Objects appearing in awareness.
When this is comprehended fully,
Everything that need be known is known.

*****

One is not found anywhere.
Yet, one is still there.
This is the Pure Subjectivity of which
Wu Hsin speaks.

*****

One need not think
To know that one is.
No effort is required
To be.
It is only within
The realm of the personal that
Doership is required.

*****

None need abide in what seems to be.
Disregard the words of Wu Hsin;
Investigate.

*****

What does the tongue taste without It?
What can the ears hear without It?
The foundation of everything is
A precondition for everything.
To rest in the foundation of everything is
To become everything.

The movement of the flag
Reveals the action of the wind.
As it always is,
The Unseen supports the seen.

*****

That which is very near is
Missed by preoccupations with
Things that are farther away.

*****

The world is not external.
The body is mere clothing on the Clothed.
Seeing this is seeing all.

*****

When the poisonous tooth is
Removed from the serpent's mouth,
The serpent can be played with like a child's toy.
When the world is seen through, then
The world can be as it is seen yet
No problems arise.

*****

The position of those living naturally is
The refusal to allocate any energy toward
Making things right or wrong.

*****

Everything is important for only as long as
One is important.

How happy was Wu Hsin to realize that
There is no permanent happiness
Found in the world.

*****

Wu Hsin can neither teach one
How to fall asleep nor
How to wake up.

*****

What happens after one's death is not different from
What was happening before one's birth.

*****

The lotus flower is produced in water.
It lives in water, yet
It is untouched by the water.
The same is said for the wise,
Living in the world.

*****

The book says This is salt.
Wu Hsin says This is salt.
Yet, one still does not know it
Until one tastes it.

*****

To reach the end of one's journey is
To reach the end of oneself.
This ending is not different from
The instant prior to the beginning.

All habitual assumptions must be examined.
Peck, peck, peck.
The chick breaks free of its shell.

*****

Clear the dust from the eyes.
Then it can be seen that
The entire world is merely
The Totality appearing as the particular.

The mind is the tool of choice to
Change What-Is into
What one thinks it should be.

*****

Things act on other things.
Conditions yield to other conditions.
Wu Hsin takes his stand outside it all.

*****

Completeness cannot be
Improved by adding or
Diminished by removing.
Completeness remains.

*****

Listening to the songs of the mind
Distracts one from What-Is,
Life.
Those with clear sight know this.
The mind may continue on, but
It has lost its hold on them.

There is no location for nowhere.
There is no location for everywhere.
You are That.

*****

Personal understanding is a distortion.
It takes What-Is and
Filters it through
The sum of personal experiences.
This is no different from
The refraction of light.
There is an appearance of light, but
It is not the true light.

*****

Wu Hsin is aware of thoughts.
Wu Hsin is aware of sensations.
Wu Hsin is aware of the objects.
Wu Hsin is aware of the world.
Wu Hsin is aware.
There is awareness, prior to Wu Hsin.

*****

Going out precedes returning.
In due course, all return.
First out, then in, then
Neither in nor out.

*****

Understanding the Mystery is
The acknowledgement that
The Mystery will always be a mystery.

The origin of all troubles,
The repository of all troubles, is
One's own imagination.
In stillness, there are
No troubles to be found.

*****

The only sin is not to know and
Not to know that one doesn't know.

*****

To relegate oneself to being
Merely an individual human is to
Confine oneself to a prison cell.
The entire universe calls out to
Those with ears that can hear it.

*****

However one believes things are,
They are different from that.

*****

Many lamps.
One light.

*****

Deeply enmeshed in the concept of one's self,
One can never know one's self.
One can only know what
One takes one's self to be.
To truly know one's self,
One must stand outside and look within.

Tsu Ma was free.
Attached to nothing,
He roamed,
He explored.
Never becoming,
Only being.
He was like the wind,
Ungraspable, uncontainable.

*****

As the tree is latent in the seed,
As the fire is latent in the wood,
All things contain their future.

*****

Nothing need be done.
Nothing need be undone.
One remains as one is.
Wu Hsin calls this the natural state.
It is the end of
Millions of beginnings and of
Millions of becomings.

*****

The fish in the ocean
Imagines itself to be
The fish on the dinner plate.
A change in the viewpoint brings about
A change in the experience.

*****

One's taste of tea is one's own only.
Likewise, one's world is one's own only.
Beyond this,
Outside of one's this and one's that,
There is the invitation of Oneness.

One can speak about
Silent mind or chattering mind.
But who speaks about the source of mind,
What resides behind the mind?
Silent mind or chattering mind are conditions.
Wu Hsin speaks only of the Unconditioned.

*****

The actuality is always now.

*****

Individuality dies with
The death of the body.
Yet, individuality can die before
The death of the body.
Wu Hsin calls the latter freedom.

*****

One cannot choose to wake up from
Either one's dreams or
One's imaginings.

*****

Before pain arrives,
That which knows the pain is present.
When pain arrives,
That which knows the pain is present.
After pain has gone,
That which knows the pain is present.
The pain is transient;
That which knows the pain,
The Knowing, is not.

Pi Dan was an expert on
All things inconsequential.
He was knowledgeable of the world, but
Of his true nature,
Of what resided at his core,
He knew nothing.

*****

One's mind is both friend and foe.
It creates the distortions yet has
The potential to see through them.
However, it is limited.
Mind cannot take one
Beyond mind.

*****

People need words until
Direct experience speaks louder.
Then, silence prevails.
It is for this reason that
Wu Hsin writes.

*****

To say I live is a distortion.
There is life.
Activities may change in every moment, but
That which supports the activities
Remains changeless.

*****

Clarity cannot be quickened.
It is already there.
It is only the veils,
The mists of thought that
Tend to obscure it.

Empty of everything,
How easy it is to be filled.

*****

At the moment of one's birth,
Death begins its pursuit.
Those who perceive themselves as not born,
As that which is eternal, are
Never caught up in
Death's net.

*****

Reject thinking.
Reject not thinking.
This is naturalness wherein
The particular becomes the universal.

*****

In true wakefulness,
There is no fear.
The prerequisite of fear is an other;
In wakefulness, this is absent.

*****

Don't take life personally.
The sun has no care for
What passes through the sky.

The I in I saw,
I remembered,
I felt, is not the person.
It is the voice of
That which moves the person and
Sustains the person.
It is That.
You are That.
In That,
One's marriage to the me is finished.
The me may remain but
Its falseness is now seen through.
When the false loses its hold,
It becomes like
The ash of a burnt rope;
It is there, but
It has no substance.

*****

A shadow is insubstantial to
The one who casts it.
When it becomes clear that
Any one is merely a shadow,
The attention returns to
The Source and rests there.

*****

Lacking labels,
Lacking definition,
One is boundless.
To reduce oneself to
The span of a lifetime and
The volume of a body is
The summit of ignorance.

Understanding is not necessary.
The end to misunderstanding is sufficient.

*****

This ever-present intelligent energy is not an experience.
It is not bound by time.
It is the underlying support from which
All experience emerges and dissolves.
To realize this as one's very nature is to
Move beyond the world.

*****

True happiness does not come and go.
True peace does not come and go.
What comes and goes is what
Obscures true happiness and true peace.

*****

Whereas the world is observable,
Whereas the person is observable,
That which observes cannot be found.
Those who have found
That which cannot be found have
Transcended both the world and the person.

*****

Within the natural order,
There are opposites but
No opposition.
All opposition is sourced from
What is not natural.

A thought arises and it is perceived.
What makes it my thought?
The bird sings and it is perceived.
Does one make it my song?

*****

Entranced by the beautiful flowers,
One misses the root which is
Clear and evident.
With the trance broken,
The fullness reveals itself.

*****

Doubt everything, even Wu Hsin.
Investigate;
Discard all that is acquired and false.
What remains is illumination itself.

*****

Wu Hsin's recipe:
Add no thing.
Take away every thing.
Bake until done.

*****

Identity is an acquired idea.
One is what one was
Prior to the acquisition.

*****

Beyond the mind,
All distinctions cease.

Lucidity is the full knowing of
Both what one appears to be and
What one truly is.

*****

Not unlike the sun,
One is that which illuminates all.
Not unlike the mirror,
One is that which reflects all.

*****

With the onset of imagination,
Space is filled with objects and
Time is filled with events.
The absence of imagination
Empties space and time so that
True peace may be perceived.

*****

Awareness itself is vastly
More important than its content.
As such, turning away from the content,
From the objective,
Turning toward the subjectivity, is
The posture of the wise.
It is only the fool who seeks
The source of things in things.

What effort is required?
The same effort that
The already wealthy man uses
To become wealthy.
What can be gained can be lost.
What cannot be gained,
Because it already is,
Can never be lost and
Requires no effort.

*****

Eternity is available in a single instant.
Turn away from one's preoccupations.
Eternity presents itself.

*****

Having rejected acceptance and
Having rejected rejection,
A clarity manifests which
Allows the world to be as it is.
There are some who would
Call this peace.

*****

When the preoccupation with identification falls away,
What is seen is that
Life is not a search for wholeness;
Rather, it is the expression of wholeness.

*****

The easiest of all things is to be
What one already is.
In that, there is nothing to attain
Nothing to gain and
No effort required.

When the seeing is unimpeded,
The totality of perfection is recognized to
Include the totality of seeming imperfections.

*****

What is false need not be remedied.
It merely needs to be seen as false.

*****

When all the stories have been discarded,
What becomes evident is that
One ends where one begins,
In the infinite expanse of the Absolute.

*****

The world and
The awareness of the world is like
Clothing and nakedness:
The nakedness is always present;
The clothing simply obscures it.

*****

A deepening of understanding requires
A shallowness of understanding.
There is no deepening to deep understanding.

*****

What one is is this pristine awareness.
All that appears on it, in it, is
Merely passing through.
Why give it importance?

The cage of being fractional
Can be replaced in an instant by
Seeing the expanse that one truly is.
All one need do is stop and look.

*****

Inadvertence imprisons.
Attention liberates.

*****

As the statue is already present in the granite,
So too, what is sought is already present.
As the carver cuts the stone,
Carve away the obstructions and
The sought appears.

*****

There is no goal.
If there is no goal to be attained,
What need one do?

*****

Prior to all form,
Prior to all names,
There is some thing,
Which is no thing that
Perceives all names and all forms.
You are That.

In the same tree,
Leaves, flowers, berries and branches,
All different from one another, are seen.
Are they not one
Because their root is the same?
Are they not all tree?

*****

Sam Fu used to think that he thought.
Upon investigation, he discovered that
Thoughts arise in the expanse of awareness and that
There is no thinker thinking.
Sam Fu now watches the show as
A spectator in the audience.
He may laugh.
He may cry.
He carries on his normal activities.
Yet never forgets That which facilitates and is
The support of these activities.

*****

Some ask that It be explained.
What can be said about It other than
It is neither this nor that.
It is That from which
This and that emerge.

*****

What Wu Hsin knows is valueless.
All that is valuable is
One's own knowing.
Although Wu Hsin may take one to the river,
He cannot make one swim.

Translations of Wu Hsin by Roy Melvyn